The Story of a Special Day
Volume 69

March 9

68th day of the year
(69th in leap years)
297 days remaining
until the end of the year.

by Michael Dobson

Timespinner
Press

For more information about the series, about me, or about your special day, please email us at editor@timespinnerpress.com.

Look for other volumes in *The Story of a Special Day,* coming often.

Table of Contents

March 9 Quotations

"All mankind is from Adam and Eve: an Arab has no superiority over a non-Arab nor a non-Arab has any superiority over an Arab; also a white has no superiority over black nor a black has any superiority over white except by piety and good action."

— The Last Sermon of the Prophet Muhammad, delivered March 9, 632 CE

"The trouble with free elections is that you never know how they are going to to turn out."

— Vyacheslav Molotov, born March 9, 1890

"I have come to the conclusion, after many years of sometimes sad experience, that you cannot come to any conclusion at all."

— Vita Sackville-West, born March 9, 1892

"If the public likes you, you're good. Shakespeare was a common, down-to-earth writer in his day."

— *Mickey Spillane, born March 9, 1918*

"I object to being called a chess genius because I consider myself to be an all around genius who just happens to play chess, which is rather different."

— *Bobby Fischer, born March 9, 1943*

"Work expands so as to fill the time available for its completion."

— *C. Northcote Parkinson, died March 9, 1993*

"My ambition is handicapped by my laziness."

— *Charles Bukowski, died March 9, 1994*

"Happiness is having a loving, close knit family in another city."

— *George Burns, died March 9, 1996*

Event of the Day

The Monitor and the Merrimac

The most important — and most famous — naval battle of the American Civil War goes by several names: the Battle of Hampton Roads, the Battle of Ironclads, and the Battle of the *Monitor* and the *Merrimac*. It began on March 8, 1862, and the most famous encounter of the battle took place on March 9, 1862.

In the earliest days of the war, Confederate forces seized the Gosport Shipyard in Norfolk, Virginia (now known as Norfolk Naval Shipyward), the oldest and largest military shipbuilding facility in America. It was a huge coup for the Confederacy, giving them over 1,000 heavy guns and numerous ships. However, Union naval forces controlled the entrance to the harbor, and Norfolk was almost completely cut off from the sea.

While sailing ships were still most common, some of the newer vessels used steam power, and that led ship designers to think about metal armor to protect their vessels. Both the French and the British had experimented with ironclads, but their use was still controversial.

Because the Confederacy couldn't match the number of Union ships, they decided to build armored ships to give them the military edge. They built their first "ironclad ram" ship on the skeleton of the steam-powered USS *Merrimack,* which had been partially destroyed when the Union left Norfolk. Although the new ironclad ship was commissioned as the CSS *Virginia,* the original name (minus the final "k") stuck.

Word of the Confederate program reached Union intelligence, and the Union started an ironclad program of their own. Rather than convert an existing ship, they built a brand-new design, the USS *Monitor.* Although *Virginia* was started first, the *Monitor* finished a few days before her counterpart.

On March 8, 1862, the CSS *Virginia* steamed into battle, ramming the Union blockading ship USS *Cumberland,* sinking her, and then destroying the USS *Congress* in the greatest defeat for the U.S. Navy until World War II.

Although there was panic in Washington, the Secretary of War reassured Lincoln's cabinet that the USS *Monitor* was on its way. The next morning, March 9, 1862, the *Monitor* entered Hampton Roads.

At first, the strange design of the new ship confused the Confederates, who thought it was a boiler that had come loose from a Union ship. When its true nature became known, Confederate sailors mocked it as "a cheese on a raft." But when the two ironclads engaged, no one was laughing.

The battle raged for hours, but neither vessel could overcome the other. The Confederate ship had no armor-piercing shot, and the Union vessel's guns used too little gunpowder. The battle ended when a shell from *Virginia* hit the *Monitor* pilot house, temporarily blinding the commander. *Monitor* retreated. *Virginia,* thinking she had won the battle, steamed away.

Virginia needed repairs after the battle, and by the time it was ready for service, the Union had its own ironclads on duty in the blockade. The Confederates scuttled her to keep her from falling into enemy hands. *Monitor* likewise did not survive the war; as she was being towed south, waves washed into the vessel, sinking it.

While the battle itself was far from decisive, its effects reached far beyond the Civil War. Within years, ironclad ships dominated the navies of the world.

USS *Monitor* after the battle. Notice the dents in the turret made by the guns of the *Merrimac*.

March 9 Holidays and Celebrations

Teacher's Day (Lebanon)

March 9 is celebrated as Teacher's Day (*Eid Al Moalim*) in Lebanon.

Christian Feast Days

Saints commemorated on March 9 include Catherine of Bologna, the Forty Martyrs of Sebaste, Frances of Rome, Gregory of Nyssa, and Pacian.

Gregory of Nyssa

What Happened on March 9?

632 CE - The Last Sermon of the Prophet Muhammad

On the 9th of Dhu al-Hijjah, 10 AH (March 9, 632), Muhammad preached his farewell sermon, known as خطبة الوداع, or Khuṭbatu l-Wadā, on Mount Arafat, a hill east of Mecca. When Muslims make their *hajj* pilgrimage, they spend a day on Mount Arafat praying for the forgiveness of sins.

1500 CE - The Cabral Fleet Departs Portugal

On March 9, 1500, a fleet of 13 Portuguese ships under the command of Pedro Álvares Cabral left Lisbon for the New World. Unlike the earlier Columbus expeditions, Cabral's fleet turned south, discovering the South American continent, and ultimately claiming Brazil in the name of the Portuguese crown.

Cabral sees Brazil for the first time

1566 CE - Murder of Mary Queen of Scott's Alleged Lover

On the night of March 9, 1566, a conspiracy of Protestant nobles stabbed Davide Rizzio, private secretary to Mary Queen of Scots, a total of 56 times, while the young queen, seven months pregnant, screamed hysterically. Her husband, Lord Darnley, was reputedly behind the murder. Rumors had been flying for some time that Rizzio and the queen were having an affair. Other sources suggest that Mary's cousin Queen Elizabeth I of England was behind the attack, hoping to destabilize Mary's rule.

The Murder of Rizzio, by John Opie, 1787

1841 CE - United States v. *The Amistad* Decided

In a lawsuit with international implications, the U.S. Supreme Court ruled that rebel slaves who had taken over their captors' ship, *The Amistad,* had been taken into slavery illegally and were entitled to fight back. After the Court's decision on March 9, 1841, supporters helped the freed slaves return to Africa the following year.

1847 CE - Siege of Veracruz

On March 9, 1847, the U.S. Army conducted its first large-scale amphibious assault, landing a division on Collado Beach without losing a single man. The success of this assault allowed U.S. forces to surround the city of Veracruz, beginning a 20-day siege that led to the surrender of the city.

Amphibious landing at Veracruz

1910 CE - Westmoreland County Coal Strike

One of the many deadly clashes between labor and management began on March 9, 1910, when coal miners protested a 16% cut in wages. The strike grew to cover 65 mines and over 15,000 striking workers, and lasted well over a year, punctuated by violence on the part of law enforcement. The financial toll on the union was too great, and the strike ended on July 1, 1911.

1916 CE - Pancho Villa Attacks New Mexico

Desperate for military supplies, General Pancho Villa and 100 of his revolutionary soldiers to attack military facilities in Columbus, New Mexico, on March 9, 1916. Although the raid was successful in acquiring needed supplies, nearly 80 of Pancho Villa's men were killed against 18 Americans.

1925 CE - Pink's War

Beginning on March 9, 1925, and lasting until May 1, 1925, the British Royal Air Force conducted the first air action independently of the Royal Army or Navy. British fighters strafed and bombed the mountain strongholds of Mahsud tribesmen in South Waziristan, part of modern-day Pakistan along the border with Afghanistan.

1945 CE - Operation Meetinghouse

Beginning on March 9, 1945, and continuing to the next day, the U.S. Army Air Force conducted the single most destructive and deadly bombing raid in history against the Japanese capital city of Tokyo. Over 300 B-29 Superfortress bombers dropped 1,700 tons of bombs, destroying 16 square miles of the city and killing over 100,000 people, more than were killed in either Hiroshima or Nagasaki.

1959 CE - Barbie® Debuts

At the American International Toy Fair in New York City on March 9, 1959, toymaker Mattel, Inc., premiered the Barbie® doll, the first adult-bodied mass-market doll. Barbie has become an international cultural icon, with over one billion sold worldwide.

1961 CE - Sputnik 9

The ninth Sputnik launch on March 9, 1961, was actually the first test flight of the Vostok spacecraft, which would take Soviet cosmonaut Yuri Gagarin into space a little over a month later.

1977 CE - Hanafi Siege

On March 9, 1977, twelve African-American Muslim gunmen led by Hamaas Abdul Khaalis, occupied three buildings in downtown Washington, DC. They took 149 hostages, killing two and wounding future DC mayor Marion Barry. After a 39-hour standoff, in which D.C. police were assisted by three Muslim ambassadors, the attackers surrendered. They were subsequently tried and convicted, with the ringleader receiving a sentence of 21 to 120 years.

1997 CE - Notorious B.I.G. Killed

On March 9, 1997, rapper Christopher George Latore Wallace, known as The Notorious B.I.G. and Biggie Smalls, was killed in a drive-by shooting in Los Angeles by an unknown assailant. Various theories about the murder continue to circulate.

2011 CE - Last Flight of Space Shuttle *Discovery*

After spending a cumulative total of one full year (365 days) in space, the Space Shuttle *Discovery* made its final touchdown on March 9, 2011. *Discovery,* the third operational shuttle, flew the Hubble Space Telescope into orbit. It is now on display at the National Air and Space Museum's Udvar-Hazy Center near Dulles Airport outside Washington, DC.

Space Shuttle *Discovery* takes off

Who Was Born on March 9?

The abbreviation "O.S." on some dates refers to the fact that the Russian Empire did not switch from the Julian to the Gregorian calendar at the same time as the rest of Europe, and therefore some figures have two dates for their birth or death.

People whose original names are not in the Western alphabet have their native names in the appropriate script shown in parenthesis.

Acting

Brittany Snow (March 9, 1986 —)

Actress Brittany Snow appeared on the soap opera *Guiding Light* and in various films and prime time shows.

Ben Mulroney (March 9, 1976 —)

Son of former Canadian prime minister Brian Mulroney, Ben Mulroney co-anchors the weekend edition of *Good Morning America*.

Kerr Smith (March 9, 1972 —)

Kerr Smith played featured roles on *Dawson's Creek* and *Charmed*, in addition to movie roles.

Jean Louisa Kelly (March 9, 1972 —)

Jean Louisa Kelly is best known as Kim Warner on the long-running sitcom *Yes, Dear*.

Emmanuel Lewis (March 9, 1971 —)

Emmanuel Lewis played the title character in the 1980s sitcom *Webster*.

Emmanuel Lewis

Juliette Binoche (March 9, 1964 —)

French actress Juliette Binoche won an Academy Award for her role in 1996's *The English Patient*.

Tom Amandes (March 9, 1959 —)

Actor Tom Amandes played Eliot Ness in the 1990s version of *The Untouchables* TV series.

Linda Fiorentino (March 9, 1958 —)

Actress Linda Fiorentino won Best Actress awards from the New York Film Critics Circle and the London Film Critics Circle for her role in 1994's *The Last Seduction.*

Ornella Muti (March 9, 1955 —)

Italian actress Ornella Muti is best known to English-speaking audiences as Princess Aura in 1980's *Flash Gordon* and for her role in 1992's *Once Upon a Crime.* She was voted "The Most Beautiful Woman in the World" in 1994, and famously insured her breasts for $350,000.

Jamie Lyn Bauer (March 9, 1949 —)

Jamie Lyn Bauer is best known for her two long-running soap opera roles as Lorie Brooks on *The Young and the Restless* and as Laura on *Days of Our Lives.*

Trish Van Devere (March 9, 1943 —)

Actress Trish Van Devere starred on *One Life to Live* and appeared in numerous movies and television shows, often with her husband, George C. Scott.

Raúl Juliá (March 9, 1940 — October 24, 1994)

Raúl Juliá received four Tony Award nominations, two Golden Globes, and numerous other awards and nominations in his distinguished acting career.

Marty Ingels (March 9, 1936 —)

Comedian Mary Ingels co-starred in the 1962 sitcom *I'm Dickens, He's Fenster*, and has a recurring role on *The Dick Van Dyke Show*. He is also a voice artist known for many cartoon characters.

Marty Ingels (right) with John Astin

Taina Elg (March 9, 1930 —)

Finnish-American actress Taina Elg won two Golden Globe awards and was on *One Life to Live* in 1980-81.

Carl Betz (March 9, 1921 — January 18, 1978)

Actor Carl Betz is best known as Donna Reed's husband in the eponymous *The Donna Reed Show* and for his Emmy-winning role in *Judd for the Defense.*

Carl Betz (top right) with the cast of *The Donna Reed Show*

Will Geer (March 9, 1902 — April 22, 1978)

Actor Will Geer is best known for his role of Grandpa Walton on the 1970s TV series *The Waltons*.

Eddie Foy Sr. (March 9, 1856 — February 16, 1928)

Vaudevillian Eddy Foy Sr. is best known for his stage act Eddy Foy and The Seven Little Foys.

Chess

Bobby Fischer (March 9, 1943 — January 17, 2008)

Grandmaster Bobby Fisher is considered one of the greatest chess players of all time. Later in life, he became known for various anti-American and anti-semitic statements. His U.S. passport was revoked and he settled in Iceland until his death.

Bobby Fischer (left)

Crime

Dennis Rader (March 9, 1945 —)

Known as the "BTK Killer," Dennis Rader murdered ten people in and around Wichita, Kansas, between 1974 and 1991. He is serving ten consecutive life sentences for his crimes.

Ernesto Miranda (March 9, 1941 — January 31, 1976)

Ernesto Miranda's conviction on kidnapping, rape, and armed robbery was overturned by the U.S. Supreme Court because he was not informed of his right against self-incrimination in the landmark case *Miranda v. Arizona,* from which the *Miranda* warning is derived. Miranda was re-tried without the use of the excluded confession, and he was again convicted of the crimes and sentenced to 20-30 years. Following his parole, he sold autographed *Miranda* warning cards and had numerous brushes with the law, until he was killed in a knife fight during a card game.

Exploration

Yuri Gagarin (Ю́рий Гага́рин) (March 9, 1934 — March 27, 1968)

Cosmonaut Yuri Gagarin became the first human in outer space on the *Vostok 1* orbital flight, April 12, 1961.

Yuri Gagarin

Amerigo Vespucci (March 9, 1454 — February 22, 1512)

Italian explorer Amerigo Vespucci first demonstrated that Brazil and the West Indies weren't part of Asia, as Christopher Columbus had thought, but were part of a new landmass. This new world became known as "America" as a result.

Fashion

Yamila Díaz-Rahi (March 9, 1976 —)

Argentine model Yamila Diaz-Rahi appeared on the 2002 and 2006 covers for the *Sports Illustrated* swimsuit issue. She was the first Latin spokesmodel in CoverGirl history.

André Courrèges (March 9, 1923 —)

Fashion designer André Courrèges is credited with inventing the miniskirt, and is known for his 1964 "Space Age" collection featuring clothing made of PVC and metal.

Journalism

David Pogue (March 9, 1963 —)

Technology columnist and television host David Pogue hosts the PBS series *NOVA ScienceNow* and won an Emmy for technology reporting for CBS News *Sunday Morning.*

Faith Daniels (March 9, 1957 —)

Faith Daniels was news anchor for *Today* and was the first journalist to host her own national daily talk show, *A Closer Look.*

Michael Kinsley (March 9, 1951 —)

Journalist and editor Michael Kinsley is best known as co-host of television's *Crossfire.*

Charles Gibson (March 9, 1943 —)

Charles Gibson hosted *Good Morning America* from 1987 to 2006.

Military

Johnnie Johnson (March 9, 1915 — January 30, 2001)

RAF pilot Johnnie Johnson was the highest scoring Western Allied fighter ace of World War II, with 34 confirmed individual victories.

Music

Lil' Bow Wow (March 9, 1987 —)

Rapper and actor Bow Wow (formerly Lil' Bow Wow) has released seven albums and appeared in films and several television series.

Mark Lindsay (March 9, 1942 —)

Rocker Mark Lindsay is best known as the singer for the 1960s group Paul Revere and the Raiders.

Paul Revere & the Raiders
(Mark Lindsay standing, second from the left)

John Cale (March 9, 1942 —)

Founding member of The Velvet Underground, musician John Cale has a distinguished solo career with over 30 albums.

Mickey Gilley (March 9, 1936 —)

Country singer Mickey Gilley's hits include *Room Full of Roses, Don't the Girls All Get Prettier at Closing Time,* and a remake of *Stand By Me,* featured in the movie *Urban Cowboy.* He is a cousin of Jerry Lee Lewis and Jimmy Swaggart.

Lloyd Price (March 9, 1933 —)

R&B vocalist Lloyd Price's first recording "Lawdy Miss Claudy" became a hit in 1952, followed by such songs as "Stagger Lee" and "Personality." He was inducted into the Rock and Roll Hall of Fame in 1998.

Samuel Barber (March 9, 1910 — January 23, 1981)

American composer Samuel Barber is one of the most celebrated classical composers of the 20th century. He won the Pulitzer Prize for music twice.

Politics

Bobby Sands (March 9, 1954 — May 5, 1981)

Member of the Provisional Irish Republican Army and the British Parliament, Bobby Sands died in prison while leading a hunger strike of fellow IRA prisoners.

Bernard Landry (March 9, 1937 —)

Leader of the Parti Québécois from 2001 to 2005, Bernard Landry served as premier of Quebec from 2001 to 2003.

Zillur Rahman (মোঃ জিল্লুর রহমান) (March 9, 1929 —)

Zillur Rahman was the 19th president of Bangladesh.

Desmond Hoyte (March 9, 1929 — December 22, 2002)

Desmond Hoyte was the third prime minister and the third president of Guyana.

James L. Buckley (March 9, 1923 —)

Senator and judge James Buckley challenged the constitutionality of a campaign spending law and introduced legislation to protect student records and student privacy. He is the brother of William F. Buckley Jr., founder of the conservative magazine *National Review.*

George Lincoln Rockwell (March 9, 1918 — August 25, 1967)

Founder of the American Nazi Party and a leading white supremacist, George Lincoln Rockwell was assassinated by an ex-member of his own party.

Vyacheslav Molotov (Вячесла́в Мо́лотов) (March 9 [O.S. February 25], 1890 — November 8, 1986)

Soviet politician Vyacheslav Molotov was Minister of Foreign Affairs from 1939 to 1949, negotiating the Molotov-Ribbentrop non-aggression pact, and later served as First Deputy Premier under Joseph Stalin. He was in charge of the Soviet atomic bomb project and contributed music to the Soviet national anthem. He is the namesake of the "Molotov cocktail," used by Finns in their fight against the Soviets during the Winter War.

David Davis (March 9, 1815 — June 26, 1886)

Illinois senator and Supreme Court justice David Davis was Abraham Lincoln's campaign manager at the 1860 Republican National Convention and helped engineer Lincoln's nomination for the Presidency.

Religion

Aloysius Gonzaga, S.J. (March 9, 1568 — June 21, 1591)

Jesuit Aloysius Gonzaga was canonized in 1726 and named the patron saint of young students. His feast day is celebrated on June 21, the day of his death.

Saint Aloysius Gonzaga by Francisco de Goya

Science and Engineering

Gerald Bull (March 9, 1928 — March 22, 1990)

Canadian artillery designer Gerald Bull designed the Project Babylon "supergun" for the Iraqi government, and worked on a project to launch a satellite using a huge artillery piece. He was assassinated in 1990. Both Iran and Israel are suspected of the assassination.

Walter Kohn (March 9, 1923 —)

Walter Kohn shared the Nobel Prize in chemistry in 1998 for his work in understanding the electronic properties of materials.

Paul Klipsch (March 9, 1904 — May 5, 2002)

Audio pioneer Paul Klipsch developed the Klipschorn, the first speaker to faithfully reproduce the sound of a live orchestra inside the home.

Sports

Julia Mancuso (March 9, 1984 —)

U.S. Ski Team racer Julia Mancuso won a gold medal at the 2006 Winter Olympics and two silver medals at the 2010 Winter Olympics.

Antonio Bryant (March 9, 1981 —)

Former college All-American wide receiver Antonio Bryant played for Dallas, Cleveland, San Francisco, and Tampa Bay.

Aaron Boone (March 9, 1973 —)

Infielder Aaron Boone's famous home run won the 2003 American League Championship Series for the New York Yankees. He is a game analyst for ESPN's *Baseball Tonight*.

Mahmoud Abdul-Rauf (March 9, 1969 —)

Considered one of the greatest free-throw shooters in the history of basketball, Mahmoud Abdul-Rauf is also known for his refusal to stand for the American national anthem and for calling the U.S. flag a symbol of oppression.

Benito Santiago (March 9, 1965 —)

Puerto Rican catcher Benito Santiago played twenty seasons in Major League Baseball, and was considered the premier catcher in the National League during his prime.

Brian Bosworth (March 9, 1965 —)

Two-time All-American linebacker Brian Bosworth played for the Seattle Seahawks, and was known for his outspoken and controversial persona. He was later named the sixth worst flop in the last 25 years by ESPN in 2004.

Phil Housley (March 9, 1964 —)

American hockey player Phil Housley is the second leading scorer among U.S.-born players, and was named to the United States Hockey Hall of Fame in 2004.

Rick Steiner (March 9, 1961 —)

Wrestler Rick Steiner was a United States Heavyweight Champion and an eight-time World Tag Team Champion in his WCW career.

Danny Sullivan (March 9, 1950 —)

Racer Danny Sullivan won the 1985 Indianapolis 500.

Doug Ault (March 9, 1950 — December 22, 2004)

First baseman Doug Ault is best known for hitting the first two home runs in the Toronto Blue Jays MLB franchise history.

Tom Sestak (March 9, 1936 — April 3, 1987)

Buffalo Bills lineman Tom Sestak was a three-time All-American selection and holds a shared record for holding opposing rushers without a touchdown for seventeen consecutive games.

Marlene Streit (March 9, 1934 —)

Canadian Marlene Streit was elected to the World Golf Hall of Fame in 2004. She is the only golfer to have won the Australian, British, Canadian, and U.S. Women's Amateurs.

Writing

Keri Hulme (March 9, 1947 —)

New Zealand author Keri Hulme won the Booker Prize for her 1984 novel *The Bone People*.

Mickey Spillane (March 9, 1918 — July 17, 2006)

Crime novelist Mickey Spillane sold over 225 million books, and in 1980 had written seven of the top 15 all-time best-selling fiction titles in the U.S.. He was best known for his detective character Mike Hammer.

Vita Sackville-West (March 9, 1892 — June 2, 1962)

Author and poet Vita Sackville West is famous for her novels *The Edwardians* and *All Passion Spent,* and for her long affair with Virginia Woolf, which inspired Woolf's novel *Orlando.*

Taras Shevchenko (Тарас Шевченко) (March 9 [O.S. February 25], 1814 — March 10 [O.S. February 26], 1861)

Ukrainian poet and artist Taras Shevchenko is considered to be the founder of modern Ukrainian literature and even the modern Ukrainian language. He was also known for his painting and illustration, and is memorialized throughout the Ukraine.

Portrait of Vita Sackville-West by William Strang

Who Died on March 9?

Acting

Jeanette Schmid (November 6, 1924 — March 9, 2005)

Female impersonator Rudolf Schmid was known for bawdy material until he appeared before the Shah of Iran. Forced to improvise, he whistled classical compositions and toured the world as a cross-dressing whistler. Schmid underwent sex reassignment surgery in 1964 and became known as Jeanette Schmid. She was awarded the Austrian Decoration of Merit in Gold for her whistling talent.

George Burns (January 20, 1896 — March 9, 1996)

Legendary comedian George Burns successfully mastered vaudeville, film, radio, and television in his iconic career. He was married to his comedy partner Gracie Allen.

George Burns and Gracie Allen

Faye Emerson (July 8, 1917 — March 9, 1983)

Actress and interviewer Faye Emerson was known as "the first lady of television" for her numerous appearances in the early days of the medium.

Art

Robert Mapplethorpe (November 4, 1946 — March 9, 1989)

Controversial photographer Robert Mapplethorpe was best known for his highly stylized black and white photographs of flowers and nude men.

Music

Chris LeDoux (October 2, 1948 — March 9, 2005)

Country singer and rodeo champion Chris LeDoux sold over six million copies of his 36 albums and received nominations for a Grammy and an Academy of Country Music Pioneer award.

Bob Crosby (August 23, 1913 — March 9, 1993)

Bandleader Bob Crosby and his Bob-Cats were a popular act in the 1930s and 1940s. He was also the brother of singer and actor Bing Crosby.

Bob Crosby with Judy Garland

Politics

Granny D (January 4, 1910 — March 9, 2010)

New Hampshire activist Doris Haddock, known as "Granny D," walked over 3,200 miles across the United States between the ages of 88 and 90 to advocate for campaign finance reform.

John Profumo (January 30, 1915 — March 9, 2006)

British politician John Profumo's 1963 involvement with a prostitute led to the Profumo Affair, which may have helped to topple the government of Harold Macmillan.

Menachem Begin (מְנַחֵם בֵּגִין) (August 16, 1913 — March 9, 1992)

Founder of Likud and sixth prime minister of Israel, Menachem Begin shared the 1979 Nobel Peace Prize with Egyptian president Anwar Sadat.

Menachem Begin

Margot Frank (February 16, 1926 — March 9, 1945)

Sister of Anne Frank, Margot Frank died in the Bergen-Belsen concentration camp as a victim of the Holocaust.

Wilhelm I (March 22, 1797 — March 9, 1888)

Originally King of Prussia, Wilhelm I became German Emperor (Kaiser) upon the unification of Germany in 1871.

Sports

Willie Davis (April 15, 1940 — March 9, 2010)

Center fielder Willie Davis holds numerous records, including a 31-game hitting streak in 1969 that remains the longest by a Los Angeles Dodger.

Charles Bennett (December 28, 1870 — March 9, 1949)

British track and field athlete Charles Bennett won a gold medal in the 1900 Summer Olympics, the first British athlete to do so.

Writing

David Broder (September 11, 1929 — March 9, 2011)

Washington *Post* journalist David Broder was known as the dean of the Washington press corps. He made over 400 appearances on *Meet the Press* and won the Pulitzer Prize in 1973.

Terry Nation (August 8, 1930 — March 9, 1997)

Screenwriter and novelist Terry Nation is best known for creating the Daleks for *Doctor Who* and for his TV series *Blake's 7*.

A Dalek from *Doctor Who*

Charles Bukowski (August 16, 1920 — March 9, 1994)

Known as the "laureate of American lowlife," author Charles Bukowski chronicled the ordinary lives of poor Americans. He wrote the semi-autobiographical 1987 film *Barfly*.

C. Northcote Parkinson (July 30, 1909 — March 9, 1993)

Author of some sixty books, primarily related to naval history, C. Northcote Parkinson became famous for his 1958 book *Parkinson's Law,* based on his adage, "Work expands so as to fill the time available for its completion." Although intended humorously, the book made Parkinson a noted authority on public administration.

Leopold von Sacher-Masoch (January 27, 1836 — March 9, 1895)

Known in his lifetime as a utopian thinker and socialist, Leopold von Sacher-Masoch is best known today for *Venus in Furs,* a story of sexual slavery. The term "masochism" is derived from his name.

The month of March, from the illuminated manuscript *Les Très Riches Heures du duc de Berry*

March: The Third Month

In ancient Rome, March was the first month of the year. As the first month of spring, in the Mediterranean climate it marked the beginning of the military campaign season. That's why March (Martius) is named in honor of Mars, the Roman god of war.

Although the first month of the year was moved back to January sometime during the transition of Rome from a kingdom to a republic (historians differ), March was the first month of the year in Russia until the end of the 15th Century, and is the first month of the year in many other cultures and religions.

In the northern hemisphere, March 1 marks the beginning of meteorological spring. In the southern hemisphere, March is the equivalent of September, making southern hemisphere March the beginning of autumn.

March is one of the seven months that have 31 days in it. March starts on the same day of the week as November every year, and except for leap years starts on the same day as February. March starts on the same day of the week as the previous June except for leap years, and in leap years starts on the same day as the previous September and December.

March in Other Cultures

In Finland, March is called *maaliskuu* (earthy month). In Ukraine, it's *березень* (birch tree). Other names for March include *Lentmona*t (Saxon), *Hyld-monath* (Angles), and *sušec* (Slovene).

March Symbols

Birthstones: Aquamarine and bloodstone, both representing courage.

Aquamarine

Birth Flowers Daffodils

Daffodils in Bagatelle Park, Paris, France

March Events

Honorary months: Presidents, Congresses, and nations around the world issue proclamations recognizing particular months to honor certain causes. These events generally fall in March. (All US unless otherwise noted.)

- National Nutrition Month

- American Red Cross Month

- Women's History Month (celebrated in Canada during October)

- Irish-American Heritage Month

- Colorectal Cancer Awareness Month

- Fire Prevention Month (The Philippines)

Women's Suffrage picket line, 1917

"March Madness": (United States) The NCAA Men's Division I Basketball Championship, popularly known as "March Madness" or the "Big Dance," is a single-elimination tournament to establish the champion college basketball team.

Multi-day events: Some March events span multiple days.

- **Nineteen Day Fast:** (Bahá'í Faith) March 2 through March 20

Movable events: Some events change dates from year to year.

- **Commonwealth Day:** Commwealth Day, formerly Empire Day, celebrates the establishment of the Commonwealth of Nations. It is marked by a service in Westminster Abbey and by a speech by England's monarch to the Commonwealht nations around the world. Commonwealth Day is held annually on the second Monday in March, which can fall on any day between March 8 and March 14.

- **Canberra Day:** In the Australian Capital Territory, Canberra Day celebrates the official naming of Australia's capital city. It is also held annually on the second

Monday in March, which can fall on any day between March 8 and March 14.

- **Mardi Gras:** French for "Fat Tuesday," this celebration takes place the day before Ash Wednesday, the beginning of the Lenten season. The New Orleans Mardi Gras celebration is perhaps the most famous, but Mardi Gras and the Carnival season (between Ephiphany and Ash Wednesday) are celebrated in many areas with large Catholic populations. Mardi Gras can take place anywhere from February 3 to March 9.

- **Passion Sunday:** The fifth Sunday of the Christian season of Lent is known as Passion Sunday in various Protestant denominations and by some traditionalist Catholics. Sometimes, the sixth Sunday of Lent is also known as Passion Sunday, but it is more commonly known as Palm Sunday. Passion Sunday starts the two week Passiontide, which ends on Holy Saturday, the day before Easter, commemorating the day that Jesus's body was laid in the tomb. The fifth Sunday of Lent can occur as early as March 8, and as late as April 11.

Mardi Gras Night Parade, New Orleans, 2012

March Zodiac Signs

From the perspective of someone on Earth, the Sun appears to move through the sky throughout the year, along a path astronomers call the ecliptic plane. The ecliptic plane is divided into twelve constellations, known as the zodiac, based on traditionally observed patterns of stars. On your birthday, you can't see your constellation, because it's part of the daytime sky.

The zodiac was first developed by Babylonian astronomers about 2,500 years ago. Because they were unaware that the Earth wobbles like a spinning top (a motion known as *precession*), they didn't make allowance for the fact that the Sun's path through the zodiac changes over time.

That means there are now two sets of dates for your birth sign. The *tropical dates* are the original Babylonian dates; the *siderial dates* tell you where the Sun actually appears as it moves along its annual path.

Zodiac signs in March are Aquarius and Pisces.

Aquarius

Tropical January 20 to February 19

Siderial February 12 to March 8 or 9 (as late as March 10 in leap years)

Aquarius is one of the oldest recognized constellations, originally representing the Babylonian god Ea. In Latin, Aquarius means "water-carrier," represented in its symbol. In Greek mythology, Aquarius is sometimes associated with Deucalion, who survived a world-cleansing flood. In Chinese astronomy, it is known as the Black Tortoise of the North (北方玄武, Běi Fāng Xuán Wǔ).

In astrology, Aquarius is considered to be masculine and extroverted, and despite the name is an air sign. Aquarians are supposed to be philanthropical, inventive, and individualistic.

Pisces

Tropical February 20 to March 20

Siderial March 15 to April 14

In the Roman legend of Venus and her son Cupid, they escaped the clutches of Typhon, known as the "father of all monsters," by transforming into fish and tying themselves together with rope. That's why the name Pisces is plural for fish. The constellation appears as a somewhat ragged "V" shape, representing the rope, with the "fish" located at the two rope ends.

In astrology, Pisces is a water sign, compatible with the other water signs Cancer and Scorpio, as well as with the earth signs Taurus, Virgo, and Capricorn. Pisceans are supposed to be imaginative, compassionate, unworldly, secretive, and escapist.

What Day of the Week is March 9?

On what day of the week does March 9 fall?

Unfortunately, this isn't an easy question. Because the calendar year is 365 days long (366 in leap years), it doesn't divide evenly by the seven days of the week.

Also, the Earth goes around the Sun in about 365-1/4 days, so a calendar tends to drift over time. That's why the same date falls on different weekdays in different years.

This is made even more complicated by a change in calendars that took place in 1582. Our modern calendar has its roots in ancient Rome, in a calendar reform conducted by Julius Caesar. Caesar commissioned mathematicians to attack the problem, and came up with the idea of *leap years*, and thus standardized the calendar for centuries to come. This was called the *Julian calendar.*

Over time, however, the small errors in Caesar's calculation compounded. That's why Pope Gregory XIII commissioned the *Gregorian calendar*, used in most of the world today. Some countries converted in 1582, when the calendar was first developed; some converted later; other still haven't changed.

Gregorian and Julian aren't the only types of calendars. The Hebrew year, the Islamic year, and many other calendars are used in different parts of the world and among different people.

You can convert Gregorian dates to other calendars, including the Hebrew calendar, the Islamic calendar, and even the Mayan calendar by visiting the Fourmilab Calendar Converter at http://www.fourmilab.ch/documents/calendar/.

A 50-year brass perpetual calendar.

Copyright, Credit, and Contact

Follow Us

Our blog Dobson's Improbable History features short articles on events and people associated with each day, and updates several times each week. Get the latest on Twitter @SidewiseThinker.

Sources and Art Credits

All art and photographs are either in the public domain or used under a Creative Commons license. Attribution is provided where requested by the copyright owner or when of historical significance, listed below.

- The cover painting, "The Monitor and Merrimac: The First Fight Between Ironclads," was produced in 1886 by Louis Prang & Co., and is in the public domain because its copyright has expired.

- The back cover photograph of a first edition brunette Barbie® doll from 1959 (also repeated with the Barbie® entry) is used under the fair use rationale that it is (a) used for visual identification and illustration of a subject of public interest, (b) there is no free alternative, (c) it is a photograph of a 3D object that could not replace the original object and does not interfere with the copyright holder's ability to derive financial gain.

- The 1862 photograph of the USS Monitor is from the United States Naval History & Heritage Command, Photo #: NH 61923, and is in the public domain because its copyright has expired.

- The 14th century fresco of Gregory of Nyssa (original located in Chora Church) is in the public domain because its copyright has expired.

- The 1787 painting The Murder of Rizzio is by John Opie, and the original can be found in the Guildhall Art Gallery. It is in the public domain because its copyright has expired.

- The 1887 painting of Pedro Álvares Cabral seeing the coast of Brazil is by Francisco Aurélio de Figueiredo e Melo, and is in the public domain because its copyright has expired.

- The painting of the amphibious landing at the Battle of Veracruz is by N. Currier and was done in the 1840s. It is in the public domain because its copyright has expired.

- The photograph of the launch of Space Shuttle Discovery is in the public domain because it was created by NASA.

- The cropped photograph of Emmanuel Lewis was taken by a Department of Defense photographer during the 1987 event "Bob Hope's High Flying Birthday Extravaganza" and is in the public domain because it is a work of the U.S. government.

- The publicity photograph of John Astin and Marty Ingels from the television show I'm Dickens, He's

Fenster is in the public domain because it was published in the U.S. before 1977 without a copyright notice.

- The publicity photograph of the cast of The Donna Reed Show is in the public domain because it was published in the U.S. before 1977 without a copyright notice.

- The 1960 photograph of Bobby Fischer playing chess is from the 14th Chess Olympiad in Leipzig, Germany. It was taken by Ulrich Kohls, and is from the German Federal Archive (Bundearchiv Bild 183-76052-0335). It is used under the Creative Commons Attribution-Share Alike 3.0 license.

- The photograph of Yuri Gagarin is in the public domain because it was created by NASA.

- The publicity photograph of Paul Revere & the Raiders is in the public domain because it was published in the U.S. before 1977 without a copyright notice.

- The painting Consagración de San Luis Gonzaga como patrono de la juventud by Francisco de Goya was created around 1763, and is in the public domain because its copyright has expired.

- The 1918 portrait of Vita Sackville-West is by William Strang, and is in the public domain because its copyright has expired.

- The publicity photograph of George Burns and Gracie Allen is in the public domain because it was published in the U.S. before 1977 without a copyright notice.

- The screenshot of Bob Crosby and Judy Garland from the trailer for Presenting Lily Mars is in the public domain because it was published in the U.S. before 1977 without a copyright notice.

- The 1978 photograph of Menachem Begin at Andrews Air Force Base was taken by a U.S. Air Force photographer and is in the public domain because it is a work of the U.S. government.

- The 19th century chromolithograph of Kaiser Wilhelm I is in the public domain because its copyright has expired.

- The image of a Dalek from the *Doctor Who* television series is by Tony Hisgett, and is used under the Creative Commons Attribution 2.0 Generic license.

- The illustration of the month of March is from the French Gothic illuminated manuscript Les Très Riches Heures du duc de Berry by the Limbourg Brothers, Jean Colombe, and an intermediate painter whose name is lost to history.

- The photograph of aquamarine has been released into the public domain.

- The photograph of daffodils is by Myrabella, and is licensed under the Creative Commons Attribution-Share Alike 3.0 Unported license.

- The 1917 Women's Suffrage demonstration comes from the Library of Congress, Prints and Photographs Division, LC-USZ62-31799 DLC

- The photograph of the 2012 Mardi Gras Night Parade was taken by Mills Baker, licensed under the Creative Commons Attribution 2.0 Generic License. It is cropped for its use in this book.

- The 50-year perpetual calendar photograph is in the public domain.

www.ingramcontent.com/pod-product-compliance
Lightning Source LLC
Chambersburg PA
CBHW020902310526
45786CB00018B/1601